Who Grows Up on the Farm?

A Book About
Farm Animals and
Their Offspring

Written by Theresa Longenecker
Illustrated by Melissa Carpenter

Content Advisor: Julie Dunlap, Ph.D.
Reading Advisor: Lauren A. Liang, M.A.
Literacy Education, University of Minnesota
Minneapolis, Minnesota

PICTURE WINDOW BOOKS
Minneapolis, Minnesota

Editor: Peggy Henrikson
Designer: Melissa Voda
Page production: The Design Lab
The illustrations in this book were prepared digitally.

Picture Window Books
5115 Excelsior Boulevard
Suite 232
Minneapolis, MN 55416
1-877-845-8392
www.picturewindowbooks.com

Printed in the United States of America.
1 2 3 4 5 6 08 07 06 05 04 03

Library of Congress Cataloging-in-Publication Data
Longenecker, Theresa, 1955–
  Who grows up on the farm? : a book about farm animals and their offspring / written by Theresa
Longenecker ; illustrated by Melissa Carpenter.
    p. cm.
  Summary: Names and describes the offspring of a cow, horse, sheep, goat, pig, chicken, goose, and
turkey.
  ISBN 1-4048-0029-8 (lib. bdg. : alk. paper)
  1. Domestic animals—Infancy—Juvenile literature. 2. Domestic animals—Juvenile literature.
[1. Domestic animals—Infancy.] I. Carpenter, Melissa, ill. II. Title.
  SF75.5 .L66 2003
  636'.07—dc21
                                                                                    2002006282

Moooo! Oink, oink!
Peep, peep! Honk!
It's noisy on the farm.
Many animals grow up
on a farm. Some babies
stay near their mothers for a
long time. Others soon go off on their own.

Let's read about some of the baby animals
that grow up on farms.

Calf

A baby cow is called a calf.

This hungry calf drinks milk from its mother. Its legs are still a bit wobbly. Soon the calf will be stronger. Then it can jump and run around its pen.

Chick

Baby chickens are called chicks.

Chicks are wet when they hatch from their eggs, but soon they are dry and fluffy. Chicks find their own food. They peck and scratch the ground for insects and seeds to eat.

Did you know?
A newly hatched chick has a sharp bump on the top of its beak called an egg tooth. The chick uses it to break out of the egg. The egg tooth falls off soon after the chick hatches.

Lamb

A baby sheep is called a lamb.

Lambs tire easily and like to cuddle up for a nap in the straw. Then it's time to leap and play. The lambs look like their mother, but their wool coats are curlier.

Foal

A baby horse is called a foal.

Look at this foal's large eyes. A foal can see very well as soon as it is born. It has a good sense of smell, too. A foal can pick out its mother by her smell.

Gosling

A baby goose is called a gosling.

Goslings follow their mother everywhere. They are born with flaps of skin between their toes. These webbed feet help them swim just a few days after hatching.

Did you know?
Newborn goslings have tiny feathers that are soft and fluffy. These feathers are called down. Two months after hatching, a gosling has the feathers it needs to fly.

13

Kid

A baby goat is called a kid.

When kids play, they butt each other with their heads. Goat kids can run and jump when they are just hours old. They are friendly and like to be around other goats.

Piglet

A baby pig is called a piglet.

When a piglet is born, it is tiny. It drinks its mother's milk and grows fast. In a week, the piglet's weight will double. A curly tail is a sign of a healthy piglet.

Did you know?
Like their parents, piglets can't sweat to cool themselves. On hot days, they cool off by rolling in mud puddles.

Poult

A baby turkey is called a poult.

A poult does not look like its parents.
It looks more like a big chick. A poult
finds food on its own, but it stays with
its mother until it is almost one year old.

Fast Facts

Cow: Cows are female cattle, and bulls are the males. Sometimes a cow has twins, but usually only one calf is born at a time. Calves weigh about 10 times what a human newborn baby weighs. Calves drink their mother's milk. Many people drink cow's milk, too.

Chicken: Chicks are many different colors, because there are many different kinds of chickens. Chicks are often yellow, but they might be brown, white, black, gold, or a mix of these colors. Like their parents, chicks have pointed beaks to pick up food but little or no sense of smell. They have to look around to find their food.

Sheep: There are hundreds of different kinds of sheep in the world. They might be white, black, brown, or tan. Many newborn lambs weigh about the same as a newborn human. The mother can pick out her lamb from the rest of the flock by the baby's smell. Each baby knows its mother, too.

Horse: A newborn foal has long, thin legs and has trouble standing up right away. The mother gives her baby a little push to help. Within an hour or two, the foal will be able to stand. A foal looks very much like its mother, though it may be a different color. It has a shorter mane and tail than its parents, but the foal's mane and tail will grow longer.

Goose: The mother goose sits on the eggs while the father goose keeps enemies away. A little wetness under the mother's feathers helps keep the eggs just the right temperature. Because a goose's eyes are on the sides of its head, the goose can't see what is right in front of it. The goose uses its bill to feel for food and turns its head to look at things.

Goat: Mother goats usually have twins, but sometimes three kids are born at one time. A kid is born with all its hair and with its eyes open. Kids drink their mother's milk. When they grow up, they usually eat hay and grass. But goats will try to eat almost anything. Goats come in many kinds and colors: white, black, gray, brown, or reddish brown. Some people like to drink goat's milk and eat goat cheese.

Pig: Piglets are born 6 to 12 in a litter. Different kinds of pigs are different colors. Many are pink, but some are white, black, or a mix of these colors. A piglet's nose is called a snout. Pigs use their snouts to dig in the dirt for roots and insects. Usually, pigs get fat only if people feed them too much.

Turkey: A turkey hen lays about 10 speckled eggs in her nest. After they hatch, the poults follow their mother. Turkeys have great eyesight and hearing, but they can't smell very well. The long, red flap of skin that grows from a turkey's forehead over its beak is called a snood.

Farm Babies at a Glance

Word for Baby	Animal	Born How	First Food	Word for Female	Word for Male	Word for Group
Calf	Cow	Live	Mother's milk	Cow	Bull	Herd
Chick	Chicken	Egg	Grains, bugs	Hen	Rooster	Peep
Lamb	Sheep	Live	Mother's milk	Ewe	Ram	Flock
Foal	Horse	Live	Mother's milk	Mare	Stallion	Herd
Gosling	Goose	Egg	Grains, bugs	Goose	Gander	Gaggle
Kid	Goat	Live	Mother's milk	Doe	Buck	Herd
Piglet	Pig	Live	Mother's milk	Sow	Boar	Herd
Poult	Turkey	Egg	Grains, seeds	Hen	Tom	Rafter

Words to Know

beak — a bird's mouth. A chicken's beak is hard and pointed.

bill — another word for a bird's mouth. A goose uses its bill to feel for food.

butt — to hit something with the head or horns

down — the soft, fluffy feathers of a bird

egg tooth — a sharp bump on the top of a chick's beak used to break out of the eggshell

litter — a group of animals born at the same time to the same mother

mane — the long, thick hair on the back of the head and neck of a horse

snout — the long, front part of an animal's head that includes its nose, jaws, and mouth

webbed feet — animal feet with wide flaps of skin between the toes. Webbed feet help an animal paddle when it swims.

Farm Animals and the Sounds They Make

Cow	mooo
Chicken	
Hen	cluck, cluck
Rooster	cock-a-doodle-doo
Chicks	peep, peep
Sheep	baaa
Horse	naaay (or neigh)
Goose	honk
Gosling	quack, quack
Goat	m-a-a-a
Pig	oink, oink (also squeals, when excited or scared)
Turkey	
Tom	gobble, gobble
Hen	click, click
Poult	wheep, wheep (a loud, high sound)

To Learn More

Index

At the Library

Brady, Peter. *Sheep*. Mankato, Minn.:
 Bridgestone Books, 1996.

Macken, JoAnn Early. *Farm Animals*.
 Milwaukee, Wis.: Gareth Stevens
 Pub., 2002.

National Geographic Society. *National
 Geographic Animal Encyclopedia*. Washington,
 D.C.: National Geographic Society, 2000.

Stone, Lynn M. *Chickens Have Chicks*.
 Minneapolis: Compass Point Books, 2000.

On the Web

Want to learn more about baby animals?
Visit FACT HOUND at *http://www.facthound.com*.